This coloring book belongs to:

_____

_____

_____

Author's note: I do not capitalize the name "satan," because I do not ascribe him even that small honor.

God Loves You!

I pray this scripture coloring book blesses you as you color along and reflect on the promises of God! Remember, God's Word is always true! It says in 2 Corinthians that " For no matter how many promises God has made they are yes..!"

I want to encourage you, no matter what situation you may be facing, God is a God who keeps all of His promises.

He not only loves you, but He has an amazing plan for your life! I am confident as you continue to focus on God's Word you will find encouragement, peace and joy!

It says in Ephesians 3:20:

> *Now to him who is able to do immeasurably*
> *more than all we ask or imagine,*
> *according to his power that is at work within us.*

This is my prayer for you! I pray that you experience an Ephesians 3:30 life!

I do understand we all go through hard times, believe me, I have had my fair share of them! But, the great news is that God sent his son Jesus, who overcame the world, and gave us the ability and authority to do the same!

Trust me, with God on your side there is nothing you can't do!

To reach out to me or just catch up on the latest that's happening, hop on over to amyfreudiger.com

To order one of my other coloring books, or for a full list of encouraging resources, head on over to amazon and search: Amy Keesee Freudiger

Finely, let me leave you with this thought:

You are a masterpiece! God formed you with His hands, He gave you talents and abilities. He loves you and He is proud of you!

Your best days are ahead!
Love, Amy

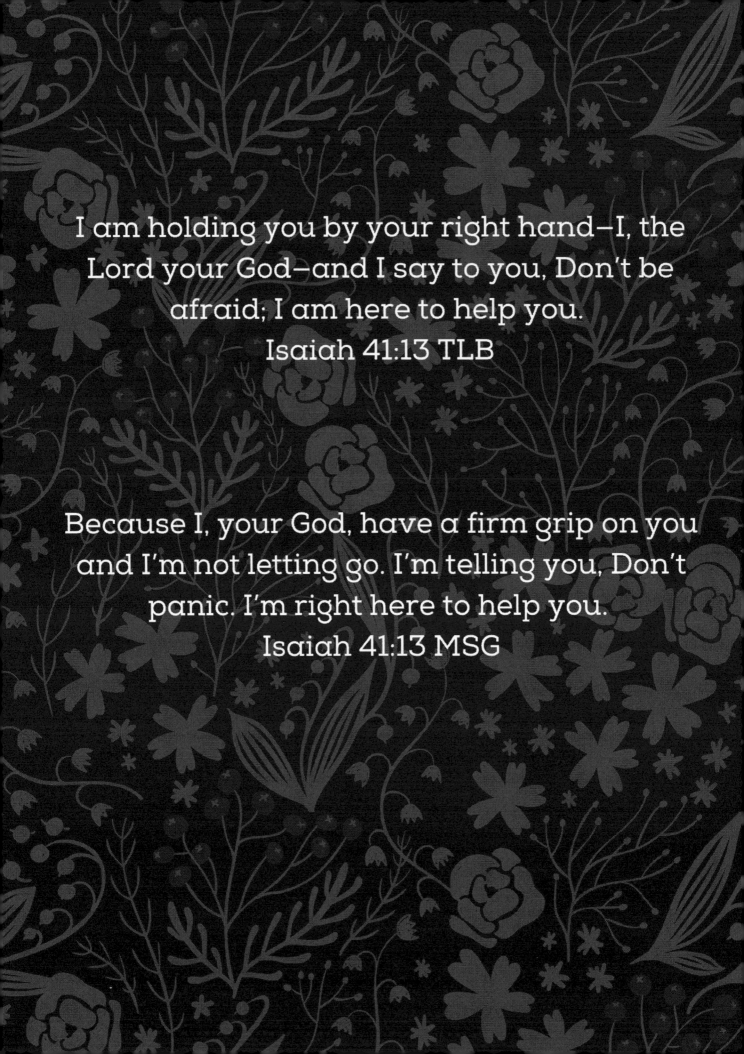

I am holding you by your right hand—I, the Lord your God—and I say to you, Don't be afraid; I am here to help you.
Isaiah 41:13 TLB

Because I, your God, have a firm grip on you and I'm not letting go. I'm telling you, Don't panic. I'm right here to help you.
Isaiah 41:13 MSG

So if the Son sets you free, you are truly free.
John 8:36 NLT

If the Son therefore shall make you free, ye shall be free indeed.
John 8:36 KJV

This is love: not that we loved God, but that he loved us and sent his Son as an atoning sacrifice for our sins.
1 John 4:10 NIV

This is love! It is not that we loved God but that He loved us. For God sent His Son to pay for our sins with His own blood.
John 4:10 NLV

Jesus said unto her, I am the resurrection, and the life: he that believeth in me, though he were dead, yet shall he live.
John 11:25 KJV

You don't have to wait for the End. I am, right now, Resurrection and Life. The one who believes in me, even though he or she dies, will live. And everyone who lives believing in me does not ultimately die at all. Do you believe this?
John 11:25 MSG

For the Lord gives wisdom; from his mouth come knowledge and understanding. He holds success in store for the upright, he is a shield to those whose walk is blameless.
Proverbs 2:6-7 NIV

For the Lord grants wisdom! From his mouth come knowledge and understanding. He grants a treasure of common sense to the honest. He is a shield to those who walk with integrity.
Proverbs 2:6-7 NLT

The Spirit Himself testifies and confirms together with our spirit [assuring us] that we [believers] are children of God.
Romans 8:16 AMP

The Spirit himself testifies with our spirit that we are God's children.
Romans 8:16 NIV

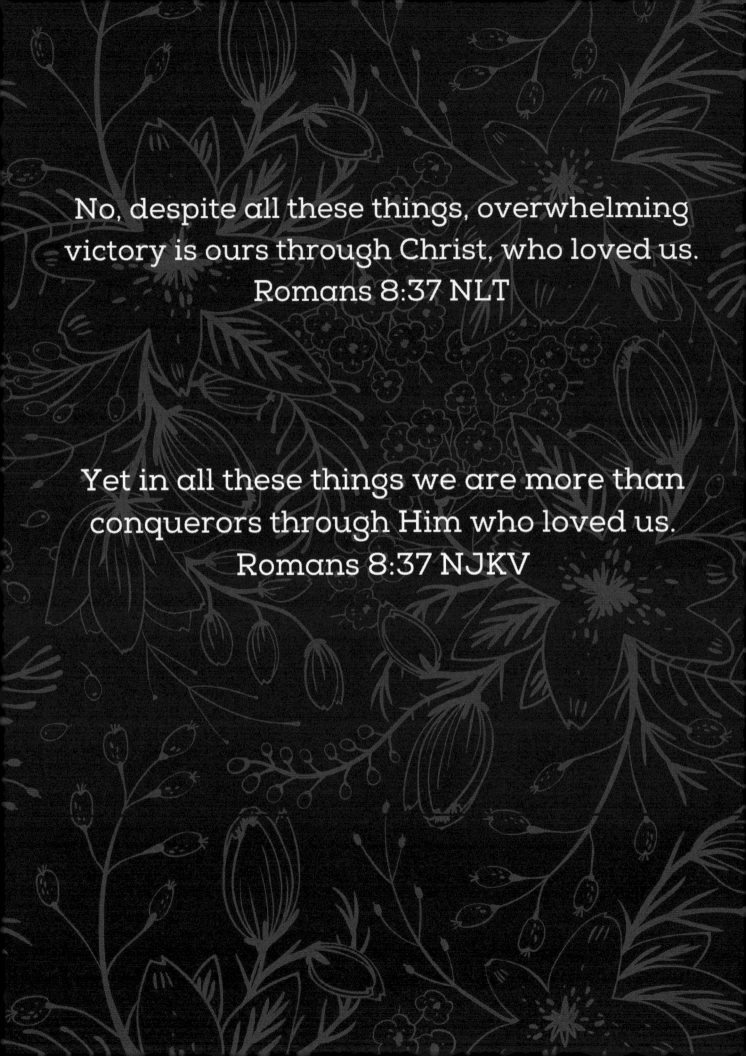

No, despite all these things, overwhelming victory is ours through Christ, who loved us.
Romans 8:37 NLT

Yet in all these things we are more than conquerors through Him who loved us.
Romans 8:37 NJKV

A thousand may fall at your side, And ten thousand at your right hand; But it shall not come near you.
Psalm 91:7 NKJV

Though a thousand fall at my side, though ten thousand are dying around me, the evil will not touch me.
Psalm 91:7 TLB

For God has not given us a spirit of fear, but of power and of love and of a sound mind.
2 Timothy 1:7 NKJV

For God did not give us a spirit of timidity or cowardice or fear, but [He has given us a spirit] of power and of love and of sound judgment and personal discipline [abilities that result in a calm, well-balanced mind and self-control].
2 Timothy 1:7 AMP

And I will ask the Father, and he will give you another Advocate, who will never leave you. He is the Holy Spirit, who leads into all truth. The world cannot receive him, because it isn't looking for him and doesn't recognize him. But you know him, because he lives with you now and later will be in you.
John 14:16-17 NLT

If you love me, show it by doing what I've told you. I will talk to the Father, and he'll provide you another Friend so that you will always have someone with you. This Friend is the Spirit of Truth. The godless world can't take him in because it doesn't have eyes to see him, doesn't know what to look for. But you know him already because he has been staying with you, and will even be in you!
John 14:16-17 MSG

If you want to know what God wants you to do, ask him, and he will gladly tell you, for he is always ready to give a bountiful supply of wisdom to all who ask him; he will not resent it.
James 1:5 TLB

If any of you lacks wisdom [to guide him through a decision or circumstance], he is to ask of [our benevolent] God, who gives to everyone generously and without rebuke or blame, and it will be given to him.
James 1:5 AMP

Every good and perfect gift is from above, coming down from the Father of the heavenly lights, who does not change like shifting shadows.
James 1:17 NIV

Whatever is good and perfect is a gift coming down to us from God our Father, who created all the lights in the heavens. He never changes or casts a shifting shadow.
James 1:17 NLT

I have given you authority to trample on snakes and scorpions and to overcome all the power of the enemy; nothing will harm you.
Luke 10:19 NIV

Listen carefully: I have given you authority [that you now possess] to tread on serpents and scorpions, and [the ability to exercise authority] over all the power of the enemy (satan); and nothing will [in any way] harm you.
Luke 10:19 AMP

For it is by grace you have been saved,
through faith—and this is not from
yourselves, it is the gift of God— not by
works, so that no one can boast.
Ephesians 2:8-9 NIV

For by grace you have been saved through
faith, and that not of yourselves; it is the gift of
God, not of works, lest anyone should boast.
Ephesians 2:8-9 NKJV

Peace I leave with you; My [perfect] peace I give to you; not as the world gives do I give to you. Do not let your heart be troubled, nor let it be afraid. [Let My perfect peace calm you in every circumstance and give you courage and strength for every challenge.]
John 14:27 AMP

I am leaving you with a gift—peace of mind and heart. And the peace I give is a gift the world cannot give. So don't be troubled or afraid.
John 14:27 NLT

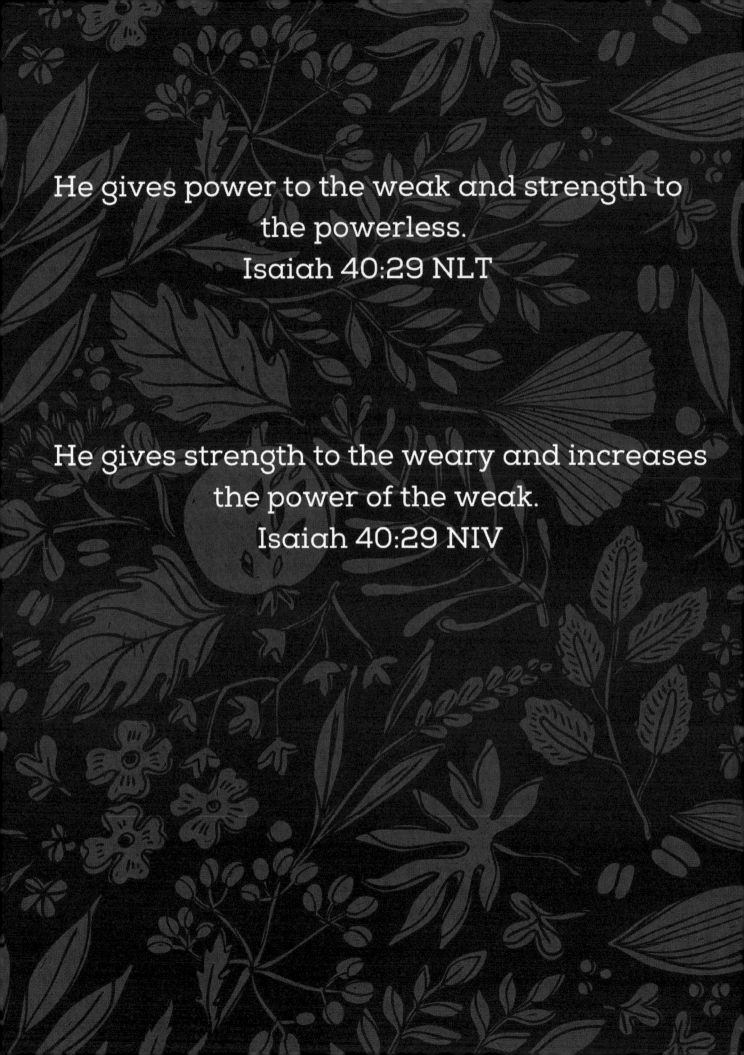

He gives power to the weak and strength to the powerless.
Isaiah 40:29 NLT

He gives strength to the weary and increases the power of the weak.
Isaiah 40:29 NIV

For sin shall no longer be your master, because you are not under the law, but under grace.
Romans 6:14 NIV

For sin will no longer be a master over you, since you are not under Law [as slaves], but under [unmerited] grace [as recipients of God's favor and mercy].
Romans 6:14 AMP

Teaching them to observe all things whatsoever I have commanded you: and, lo, I am with you always, even unto the end of the world. Amen.
Matthew 28:20 KJV

And then teach these new disciples to obey all the commands I have given you; and be sure of this—that I am with you always, even to the end of the world.
Matthew 28:20 TLB

For God so [greatly] loved and dearly prized the world, that He [even] gave His [One and] only begotten Son, so that whoever believes and trusts in Him [as Savior] shall not perish, but have eternal life.
John 3:16 AMP

For God so loved the world, that he gave his only begotten Son, that whosoever believeth in him should not perish, but have everlasting life.
John 3:16 KJV

And God said, Let us make man in our image, after our likeness: and let them have dominion over the fish of the sea, and over the fowl of the air, and over the cattle, and over all the earth, and over every creeping thing that creepeth upon the earth. So God created man in his own image, in the image of God created he him; male and female created he them.
Genesis 1:26-27 KJV

Then God said, "Let Us (Father, Son, Holy Spirit) make man in Our image, according to Our likeness [not physical, but a spiritual personality and moral likeness]; and let them have complete authority over the fish of the sea, the birds of the air, the cattle, and over the entire earth, and over everything that creeps and crawls on the earth." So God created man in His own image, in the image and likeness of God He created him; male and female He created them.
Genesis 1:26-27 AMP

A man's mind plans his way [as he journeys through life], But the Lord directs his steps and establishes them.
Proverbs 16:9 AMP

A man's heart plans his way, but the Lord directs his steps.
Proverbs 16:9 NKJV

Not at all! Let God be true, and every human being a liar.
Romans 3:4 NIV

Depend on it: God keeps His word even when the whole world is lying through its teeth.
Romans 3:4 MSG

For no matter how many promises God has made, they are "Yes" in Christ. And so through him the "Amen" is spoken by us to the glory of God.
2 Corinthians 1:20 NIV

For no matter how many promises God has made, they are "Yes" in Christ. And so through him the "Amen" is spoken by us to the glory of God.
2 Corinthians 1:20 AMP

Very truly I tell you, whoever obeys my word
will never see death.
John 8:51 NIV

I assure you and most solemnly say to you, if
anyone keeps My word [by living in
accordance with My message] he will indeed
never, ever see and experience death.
John 8:51 AMP

If we confess our sins, he is faithful and just to forgive us our sins, and to cleanse us from all unrighteousness.
1 John 1:9 KJV

But if we confess our sins to him, he can be depended on to forgive us and to cleanse us from every wrong. And it is perfectly proper for God to do this for us because Christ died to wash away our sins.
1 John 1:9 TLB

God
is faithful
to
forgive me

And we know [with great confidence] that God [who is deeply concerned about us] causes all things to work together [as a plan] for good for those who love God, to those who are called according to His plan and purpose.
Romans 8:28 AMP

And we know that God causes everything to work together for the good of those who love God and are called according to his purpose for them.
Romans 8:28 NLT

The Lord says, "I will guide you along the best pathway for your life. I will advise you and watch over you."
Psalm 32:8 NLT

I hear the Lord saying, "I will stay close to you, instructing and guiding you along the pathway for your life. I will advise you along the way and lead you forth with my eyes as your guide."
Psalm 32:8 TPT

Therefore I tell you, whatever you ask for in prayer, believe that you have received it, and it will be yours.
Mark 11:24 NIV

For this reason I am telling you, whatever things you ask for in prayer [in accordance with God's will], believe [with confident trust] that you have received them, and they will be given to you.
Mark 11:24 AMP

I have told you these things, so that in Me you may have [perfect] peace. In the world you have tribulation and distress and suffering, but be courageous [be confident, be undaunted, be filled with joy]; I have overcome the world. [My conquest is accomplished, My victory abiding.]
John 16:33 AMP

And everything I've taught you is so that the peace which is in me will be in you and will give you great confidence as you rest in me. For in this unbelieving world you will experience trouble and sorrows, but you must be courageous, for I have conquered the world!
John 16:33 TPT

He was wounded for our transgressions, He was bruised for our iniquities; The chastisement for our peace was upon Him, And by His stripes we are healed.
Isaiah 53:5 NKJV

"But he was pierced for our rebellion, crushed for our sins. He was beaten so we could be whole. He was whipped so we could be healed."
Isaiah 53:5 NLT

Don't worry about anything; instead, pray about everything. Tell God what you need, and thank him for all he has done. Then you will experience God's peace, which exceeds anything we can understand. His peace will guard your hearts and minds as you live in Christ Jesus.
Philippians 4:6-7 NLT

Be anxious for nothing, but in everything by prayer and supplication, with thanksgiving, let your requests be made known to God; and the peace of God, which surpasses all understanding, will guard your hearts and minds through Christ Jesus.
Philippians 4:6-7 NKJV

Be strong. Take courage. Don't be intimidated. Don't give them a second thought because God, your God, is striding ahead of you. He's right there with you. He won't let you down; he won't leave you.
Deuteronomy 31:6 MSG

Be strong and of good courage, do not fear nor be afraid of them; for the Lord our God, He is the One who goes with you. He will not leave you nor forsake you.
Deuteronomy 31:6 NKJV

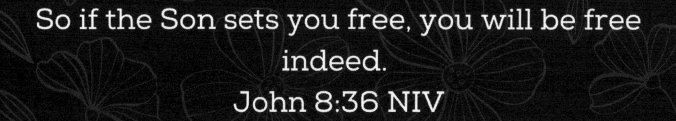

So if the Son sets you free, you will be free indeed.
John 8:36 NIV

So if the Son sets you free, you are truly free.
John 8:36 NLT

But the fruit of the Spirit is love, joy, peace, forbearance, kindness, goodness, faithfulness, gentleness and self-control. Against such things there is no law.
Galatians 5:22-23 NIV

But the fruit of the Spirit [the result of His presence within us] is love [unselfish concern for others], joy, [inner] peace, patience [not the ability to wait, but how we act while waiting], kindness, goodness, faithfulness, gentleness, self-control. Against such things there is no law.
Galatians 5:22-23 AMP

For I know the plans I have for you, declares the Lord, plans to prosper you and not to harm you, plans to give you hope and a future.
Jeremiah 29:11 NIV

For I know the plans and thoughts that I have for you, says the Lord, plans for peace and well-being and not for disaster, to give you a future and a hope.
Jeremiah 29:11 AMP

I will instruct you and teach you in the way you should go; I will counsel you with my loving eye on you.
Psalm 32:8 NIV

I will instruct you and teach you in the way you should go; I will guide you with My eye.
Psalm 32:8 NKJV

I am convinced and confident of this very thing, that He who has begun a good work in you will [continue to] perfect and complete it until the day of Christ Jesus [the time of His return].
Philippians 1:6 AMP

Being confident of this, that he who began a good work in you will carry it on to completion until the day of Christ Jesus.
Philippians 1:6 NIV

The thief comes only to steal and kill and destroy; I have come that they may have life, and have it to the full.
John 10:10 NIV

The thief's purpose is to steal and kill and destroy. My purpose is to give them a rich and satisfying life.
John 10:10 NLT

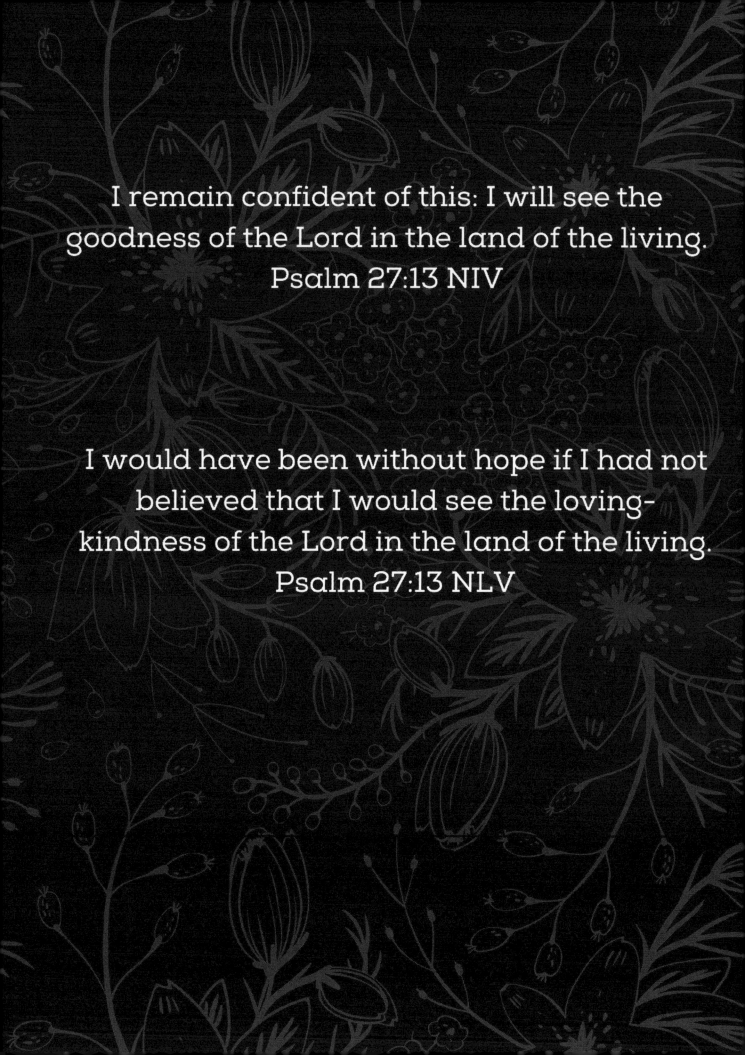

I remain confident of this: I will see the goodness of the Lord in the land of the living.
Psalm 27:13 NIV

I would have been without hope if I had not believed that I would see the loving-kindness of the Lord in the land of the living.
Psalm 27:13 NLV

So I say to you: Ask and it will be given to you; seek and you will find; knock and the door will be opened to you. For everyone who asks receives; the one who seeks finds; and to the one who knocks, the door will be opened.
Luke 11:9-10 NIV

And so I tell you, keep on asking, and you will receive what you ask for. Keep on seeking, and you will find. Keep on knocking, and the door will be opened to you. For everyone who asks, receives. Everyone who seeks, finds. And to everyone who knocks, the door will be opened.
Luke 11:9-10 NLT

But the Lord is faithful, who will establish you and guard you from the evil one.
2 Thessalonians 3:3 NKJV

But the Lord is faithful, and He will strengthen you [setting you on a firm foundation] and will protect and guard you from the evil *one*.
2 Thessalonians 3:3 AMP

Give your burdens to the Lord. He will carry them. He will not permit the godly to slip or fall.
Psalm 55:22 TLB

Cast thy burden upon the Lord, and he shall sustain thee: he shall never suffer the righteous to be moved.
Psalm 55:22 KJV

His divine power has given us everything we need for a godly life through our knowledge of him who called us by his own glory and goodness.
2 Peter 1:3 NIV

For as you know him better, he will give you, through his great power, everything you need for living a truly good life: he even shares his own glory and his own goodness with us!
2 Peter 1:3 TLB

The name of the Lord's a strong tower; The righteous runs to it and is safe and set on high [far above evil].
Proverbs 18:10 AMP

The Lord is a strong fortress. The godly run to him and are safe.
Proverbs 18:10 TLB

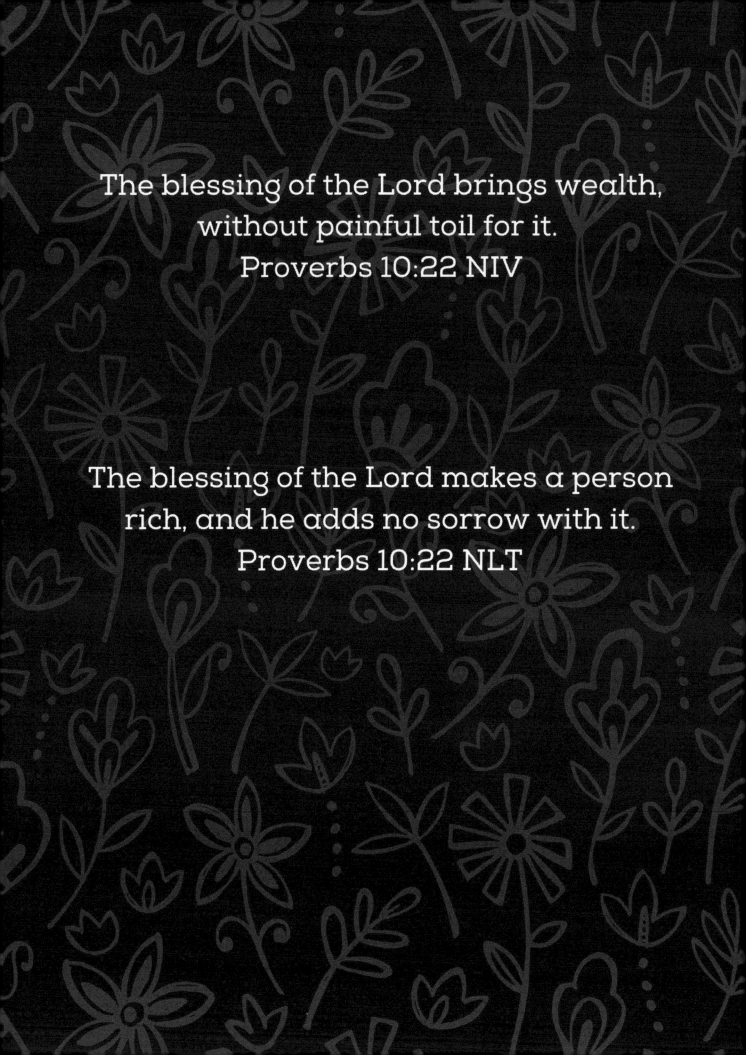

The blessing of the Lord brings wealth,
without painful toil for it.
Proverbs 10:22 NIV

The blessing of the Lord makes a person
rich, and he adds no sorrow with it.
Proverbs 10:22 NLT

When the perishable has been clothed with the imperishable, and the mortal with immortality, then the saying that is written will come true: "Death has been swallowed up in victory. "Where, O death, is your victory? Where, O death, is your sting?"
1 Corinthians 15:54-55 NIV

Then, when our dying bodies have been transformed into bodies that will never die, this Scripture will be fulfilled: "Death is swallowed up in victory. O death, where is your victory? O death, where is your sting?"
1 Corinthians 15:54-55 NLT

And so it happened just as the Scriptures say, that Abraham trusted God, and the Lord declared him good in God's sight, and he was even called "the friend of God."
James 2:23 TLB

And the scripture was fulfilled that says, "Abraham believed God, and it was credited to him as righteousness," and he was called God's friend.
James 2:23 NIV

So then you are no longer strangers and aliens [outsiders without rights of citizenship], but you are fellow citizens with the saints (God's people), and are [members] of God's household.
Ephesians 2:19 AMP

Now you are no longer strangers to God and foreigners to heaven, but you are members of God's very own family, citizens of God's country, and you belong in God's household with every other Christian.
Ephesians 2:19 TLB

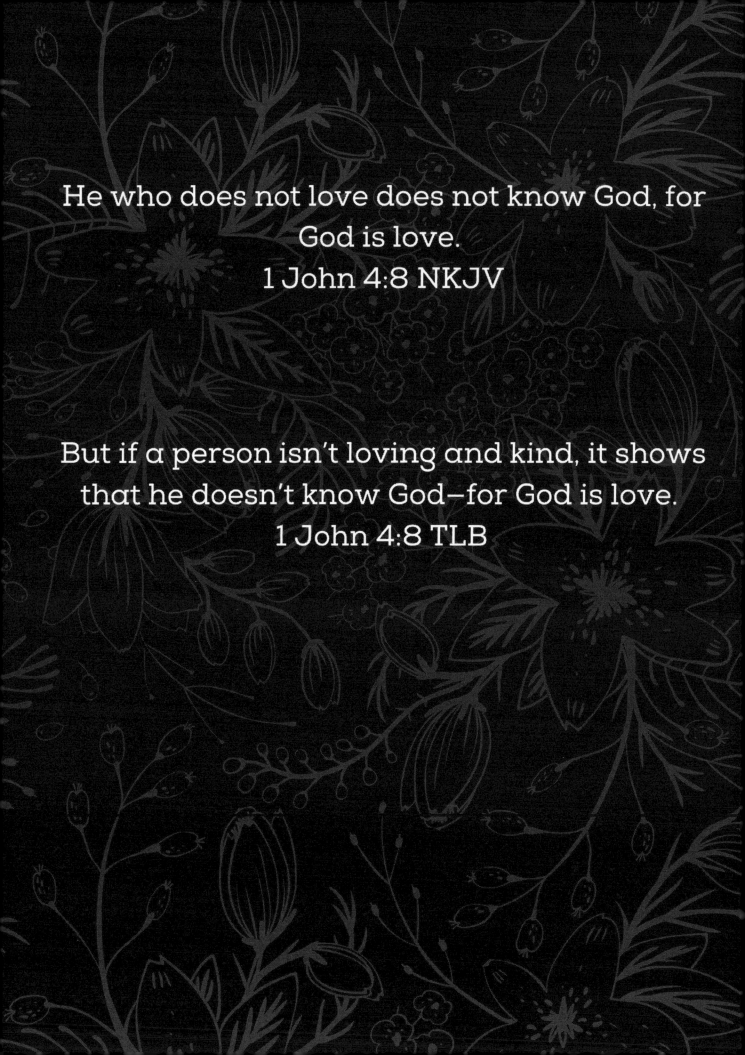

He who does not love does not know God, for God is love.
1 John 4:8 NKJV

But if a person isn't loving and kind, it shows that he doesn't know God—for God is love.
1 John 4:8 TLB

Now to him who is able to do immeasurably more than all we ask or imagine, according to his power that is at work within us.
Ephesians 3:20 NIV

Now to Him who is able to do exceedingly abundantly above all that we ask or think, according to the power that works in us.
Ephesians 3:20 NKJV